"GOOD" CHURCHES ARE GREAT
"Godly" ones are better.

And yes...there is a difference.

*"If God waited on people to become perfect
before He anointed them
to preach, teach, lead or minister,
there would never be anyone worthy,
and the work would never get done.*

*God uses willing vessels, with weaknesses,
so His strength, power, and anointing,
can shine through,
and He can get the glory!"*

Keith Hammond

Tips For Joining
A God Church

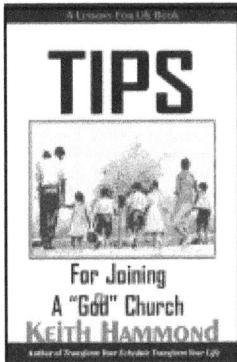

30 Things
You Should See
Under The Surface

Cover Layout and Interior Design: Keith Hammond

Lessons For Life Books

PUBLISHERS

L E S S O N S F O R L I F E B O O K S . C O M

LessonsForLifeBooks.com

▣A Lessons For Life Book

Tips For Joining
A God Church

© 2012 by
Keith Hammond
is published by
Lessons for Life Books, Inc.
7455 France Ave. S. #305
Edina, MN 55435

ISBN-13: 978-1-938588-62-4
Library of Congress Control Number: 2012915256
Printed in the U.S.A.

Dedication

God Almighty,
I give you all the glory, honor, and praise for all that you have done
and still do in, to, and through, my life.
Thank you for Jesus Christ and the Holy Spirit,
and for the redeeming power of your Love.

To my wife,
in this 28th year together,
thank you for all your prayers and patience.

To my daughters,
my Love for you goes beyond words.
Many blessings to you both.

To my grandsons,
it is a great joy
to be Blessed with your presence in our lives.

To the Hammond and Fitzpatrick families,
I pray that you will unite arm in arm one day
and allow yourselves to be encircled by
the healing power of God's Love.

To Pastor Arthur Agnew,
only God could know how grateful I am,
for the 10 years you stood by my side.
Your training and teaching and telling will always be with me.

Acknowledgement

Ken E. at MMS,
I thank God for using you to be the springboard
that helped launch this ministry.
Thank you for the open door.
I'm forever grateful.

Dana Lynn Smith
The Savvy Book Marketer
Your wisdom, knowledge & understanding,
are incredible and inspiring.
Thank you for being my coach.

There are others who at some point and time of my life,
made a measurable impact, whether good or bad,
I am thankful for your input into me,
as it helped God prune, grow and mature me in more ways,
than you will ever know.

God Bless You All.

TABLE OF ... ■ ■ ■

1
BIBLICAL 14
ANOINTED 16
GIFTED 18
PASSIONATE 20
FAITHFUL 22

2
GROWING 26
BELIEVING 30
PRAYING & FASTING 32
PRAISING & WORSHIPING 36
HONORING 40

3
LOVING 44
NURTURING 46
AGREEING 48
FORGIVING 50
COMPASSIONATE 52

4
ACCEPTING 56
HEALING 58
ADAPTING 60
HELPING 62
PARTICIPATING 64

5
UNDERSTANDING 68
LISTENING 70
TEACHING 72
TRAINING 74
READING, HEARING & DOING 76

6
CREATING 80
DEVELOPING 82
BUILDING 84
INVOLVING 86
REACHING 88

WELCOME...

to the book that may help you learn to locate a church that has the Spirit of God in it and, can show you ways to help you usher it in.

Jesus is coming back to harvest the church. That's why it's so important to be part of one. I must tell you that there is no perfect church here on Earth. It doesn't exist. So, if you're looking, stop.

This book contains information to help you identify a "Godly" church and points our key elements to help you, help yours become one.

I pray that you start, or strengthen, your relationship with one that meets both your church and ministry needs, and where you can use your own God-given gifts to help build up the church.

LIVING A CHRISTIAN LIFESTYLE IS NOT HARD, BUT IT TAKES COMMITMENT. IT TAKES HONESTY, AND DEDICATION, UNWAVERING AND UNCOMPROMISING FAITH TO RESIST A WORLD FULL OF TEMPTATION IN ORDER TO DO GOD'S WILL AND HELP REACH THOSE WHO ARE LOST IN IT OR TO HELP STRENGTHEN THOSE WHO ARE ALREADY ON THE JOURNEY.

I pray that you use this material and help others do the same. I thank God and give Him glory for using my gifts to put this book together.

In the Mighty Name of Jesus...

Amen

INTRODUCTION

Accepting the free gift of salvation is the most important decision of your life. Everything else pales in comparison to where you are going to spend eternity.

As in everything in this life, there is a process. Once you've received salvation, there is some work to do. That work, starts with joining a church. Not just any church, a "God" church. There are churches all over that do good, but I encourage people to look for a "God" church when seeking to join one. Some characteristics that identify a God church include: being Biblical, being good listeners, being adaptable in order to reach lost souls in every aspect of this ever-changing society, etc. Every "God" church has some basic characteristics that a 'good' church may not, does not, or will not have. This book helps you learn how to discern the difference.

This next statement is going to shock you, but it is the reality of what I'm about to say that holds the truth behind it. There is a church organization, yes, an entire church organization, that has a history of child molestation, which in recent years has been made known to the members, and the public. The organization, and the churches therein, do a tremendous amount of 'good' all over the world. But the one difference, and the way you can tell whether it is a 'good' church or a Godly one, is through the leadership.

Many, not just one or two, but dozens, and even hundreds, of those in this organization's leadership have been found to be something other than Godly. On the surface, they seem to be 'good' people. But, when you look inside, where it matters, years, and decades, and centuries, and generations of child molestation sits underneath.

Here's a reference point for what I just said. There are two leaders in our lives. One in Heaven; one on Earth.

The One in Heaven:
Is 'Godly' and is the model for all that is truly 'Good'.

The one on Earth:
Is bad. So bad that he was kicked out of Heaven.

The One in Heaven:
Is 'Godly' on the surface and underneath.

The one on Earth:
Looks good on the surface, but it is only a mask to cover what can never be Godly underneath.

The leadership of any church plays the most significant role in how most people perceive that church. Even if the members are raising all kinds of sand, the perception in people's minds generally always go back to the leadership.

Church leaders, whether they be pastors, priests, bishops, etc., often make untold sacrifices, but also by default, place themselves on the front line to take all the heat, blame, darts, etc.

This is why it is vital to locate a "God" church. These men and women of God are responsible for being the watchmen of your soul. If they take advantage of that responsibility, you can rest assured that God Himself will deal with them at some point.

11

So, if you're not in a God church, and you know it in the pit of your stomach, in the depth of your soul, because you see, hear, and feel things that just should not be happening in a church, beware. I'm not talking about a one-time event, but repeated occurrences of the same issues, over and over, year after year, without anyone either standing up and speaking up, or any change being made.

There is no growth in denial. But there is growth in deliverance. Whether you're seeking a God church, or believe you're already in one. Choose wisely, because you very soul is at stake. God Bless you and keep you.

12

This book is designed for you to learn something.	After each Chapter It Asks Did You Learn Anything? Share Your Answers At Blog.LessonsForLifeBooks.com

CHAPTER

one

BIBLICAL

A "God" Church Must Be Biblical. This is the number one rule. But how do you tell if your church is Biblical? By just listening and watching how the church responds to different situations. If the teaching is worldly, the response to certain situations will most likely be worldly. If the teaching is Biblical, the response to certain situations will most likely be Biblical.

A Biblical Church follows the leading of the Holy Spirit. The ultimate goal for all churches should be to win souls for Christ. Proverbs 11:30 says "He who wins souls is wise." Over 2000 years ago, Jesus gave us the great commission to go into all the world to preach and teach the gospel, share its good news with the world, and make disciples of people in all nations. The same mission is true today. And churches should be leading the way.

In Apostle Paul's letter to Timothy (2nd Timothy 4:2-5) Paul handed his apostolic torch to Timothy by telling him to, "Preach the Word; be prepared in season and out of season; correct, rebuke, and encourage, with great patience and careful instruction. For the time will come when men will not put up with sound doctrine. Instead to suit their own desires, they will gather around them a great number of teachers to say what their itching ears want to hear. They will turn their ears away from the truth and turn aside to myths. But you, keep your head in all situation, endure hardship, do the work of an evangelist, perform all the duties of your ministry."

14

Paul was telling Timothy to stick to being **Biblical** in spite of the opposition he would face; he was reassuring him to stick to what works, *because* it works.

A CHURCH THAT IS NOT BIBLICAL... IS NOT A CHURCH

Can you name or identify three things that make your church Biblical, and three areas where it may not be following Biblical standards, ethics, or protocol?

15

My Church is Biblical because?

1. _____

2. _____

3. _____

My Church may not be following Biblical standards because?

1. _____

2. _____

3. _____

◤ ANOINTED

A "God" Church Must Be Anointed. This is the 2nd equally important step next to a church being Biblical. But how do you tell if your church is Anointed? By listening to the leadership. An anointed man or woman of God speaks differently than people who are not anointed. But the only way you can really hear or tell the difference is if you're listening with spiritual ears. To learn what spiritual ears are, or how to use them you should read my book, "God's Armor For The 21st Century."

People that are anointed don't act, or react the same as those in the world. Their walk is different. They are purposeful in their walk, in their talk, in their attitude and in their actions.

Churches with anointed leaders feed the spirit of the members. If you are a member of a church and your spirit is malnourished, you are probably not being fed. Just like your physical body needs several meals daily, to stay alive, your spirit must be fed also. And just like your physical body, if you feed it the wrong food, you create problems within your body. The same is true for your spirit, you must feed it the right food.

Just like your physical body feels full when it is fed and feels hungry when it isn't, your spirit knows when it has been fed and when it hasn't.

I've never physically been to the church, and I have not done research on their works, but someone who I believe is anointed is Bishop Jakes.

GOD IS THE ONLY ONE WHO CAN ANOINT A CHURCH

Can you name or identify three things that make your church Anointed, and three areas where it may not be following God's anointing and using worldly views or interpretations?

17

My Church is Anointed because?

1. _____

2. _____

3. _____

My Church may not be using God's Anointing because?

1. _____

2. _____

3. _____

GIFTED

A "God" Church Must Be Gifted. Gifts are given by the Holy Spirit. How do you tell if your church is gifted? Look at the people. Gifts are responsible for giving ordinary people the ability to be **apostles, prophets, evangelists, pastors and teachers** so that the body of Christ may be built up. Ephesians 4:11-12. **Gifts** are for your growth and for the growth of others. Romans 12:6 says, we have different gifts according to the grace given to us. If your gift is **prophesying**, use it; **serving**, serve; **teaching**, teach; if it is **encouraging**, encourage; **contributing** to the needs of others, give generously; **leadership**, govern diligently; **showing mercy**, do it cheerfully.

18

Gifts are designed to help build up the church. 1st Corinth. 14:12. It is important to recognize your gifts, and even more important that your church uses them. Whatever you are most passionate about, helps you discover your gift(s). **Gifts** are meant to be used. 1st Timothy 4:14 says not to neglect the gift that was given to you. 1st Peter 4:10 says as each one received a gift, minister it one to another as good stewards of the manifold grace of God. God's gifts and His call are irrevocable. He doesn't take them back. Romans 11:29. **Gifts** are given to us for use in church and in ministry. Including: **singing, praise dancing, musician, architect, custodian, usher, accountant, nurse** and other things we think just *come* naturally, when they are really *given* spiritually.

Maybe you've never thought about using them in the church. So, ask yourself: How can I use my gift(s) to help build up the church and bring glory to God?!

A GOD CHURCH USES THE GIFTS OF ITS MEMBERS

Can you name or identify three things that make your church Gifted, and three areas where it may not be using God's gifts in the people that are able to be used?

My Church is Gifted because?

1. _____

2. _____

3. _____

My Church may not be using God's gifts in people because?

1. _____

2. _____

3. _____

19

PASSIONATE

A "God" Church Must Be Passionate. Passion for God's people is part of what propelled Jesus into his ministry. How do you tell if your church has passion? By the way it carries out the mission of Jesus Christ; and the work of His ministry. If a church has no zeal and joy and delight in serving God, you will recognize it right away. It will seem to be dead. The worship service will seem dead, forced, and/or repetitive. Ministry work will seem nonexistent. Members will seem like they're just coming to be coming. It will seem like they are carrying on a ritual or tradition just to call it church. **Passion** for Jesus Christ, is what turned a murderous centurion named Saul, who made a living persecuting the church, into a gospel-preaching, willing to give up his life for the sake of the gospel, Apostle, named Paul.

20

If there is something you think about constantly, to the point that you can't think about anything else at times, even when you try, you probably are very passionate about it. Godly churches are **passionate** about serving God and in their relationship with His Son, Jesus Christ and in doing ministry work such as feeding the hungry, visiting the sick, ministering to prisoners, helping strangers, etc. Matthew 25:31-46. **Passion** shows the world that you are not only serious about your faith, but that you don't care who sees you praising, worshiping, praying, crying, or just being joyful about the wonderful things God has done in your life.

All the difficult times God brought us through and all the mercy He has given us! When you see this turned into passion pouring out of people in church and its ministry you know it's a Godly one.

PASSION CAN BE SEEN POURING OUT OF PEOPLE

Can you name or identify three things that make your church Passionate, and three areas where it may not be using the passion of Jesus Christ to fulfill Matthew 25:31-46?

21

My Church is Passionate because?

1. _____

2. _____

3. _____

My Church may not be Passionate because?

1. _____

2. _____

3. _____

FAITHFUL

A "God" Church Must Be Faithful. Faith is the essence of things we hope for, the evidence of things not seen (Hebrews 1:1). How do you tell if your church is faithful? Through the words and actions of the people. I've attended church with a bunch of people who are always in church, but all they ever do is speak doubt. They complain about not having enough money for this, or not being able to do that, or this isn't done right or that isn't done right. But I've never head those same people say, "I know the Lord will make a way somehow!" That's a faithful statement.

Faithful churches don't have to know when something is going to happen, they just believe it's going to happen. Faithful churches let their faith answer the door, when doubt comes knocking. Faithful churches go into prayer about every situation because they believe in the God that has all the answers. Faithful churches don't allow tragedy to overcome them because they believe in a God who can do miracles. Churches are only faithful if the people in the church have the faith to make it faithful. Faithful churches don't alter God's word to make friends with the people, they preach the gospel in its raw form and believe that it has the power to change even unfaithful people's hearts.

"I know the Lord will make a way somehow." That's the statement, the belief and the battle cry of a faithful church.

22

This cry should be coming from more than just the pastor and should be heard in nearly every situation where there is a need.

I KNOW THE LORD WILL MAKE A WAY SOMEHOW

Can you name or identify three things that make your church Faithful, and three areas where it may not be using Faith to fight fear?

23

My Church is Faithful because?

1. _____

2. _____

3. _____

My Church may not be Faithful because?

1. _____

2. _____

3. _____

24

Biblical Anointed Gifted Passionate Faithful	Chapter Two Did You Learn Anything? Share Your Revelations At Blog.LessonsForLifeBooks.com

C H A P T E R

two

GROWING

Growth in a "God" Church should be as obvious today as it was 2000 years ago. If your church is decades old and the same 20 or 50 or 100 members are the only ones coming and no new members are being added, beware. The Bible shows thousands being added to the church regularly. The same is true today and is evident in several parts of the country. Some churches that started with a few dozen members, and over time grew to a few hundred, then a few thousand, and many of them now have tens of thousands and are "Mega Churches." This is not a freak of nature. It is divine evidence of growth in "membership."

26

Another type of **growth** is "maturity." If the church is decades old and the same members have been attending Sunday school and Bible study, and are still asking the same questions about the Bible, showing no signs of growth, be careful. Remember, in Ephesians 4:11-16 Apostle Paul said "It was He who gave some to be apostles, prophets, evangelists, pastors and teachers, to prepare God's people for works of service, so that the body of Christ may be **built up**, until we all reach **unity** in the faith and in the **knowledge** of the Son of God and become **mature**, attaining to the **whole** measure of the **fullness** of Christ. Then we will **no longer be infants,** tossed back and forth by the waves, and blown here and there by the cunning and craftiness of men in their deceitful scheming.

Instead, speaking the truth in love, we will in all things **grow up** into Him who is the Head, that is, Christ. From Him the whole body, joined and held together by every supporting ligament, **grows and builds** itself up in love, as each part does its work."

That Scripture should be more than enough to help you see and recognize and also understand that **growth** in a church is a part of the process. And it is mandatory.

Let me remind you that church growth is NOT about the pastor living good. It is NOT about how much money the church has. It's NOT about how fly your website is. And it's certainly NOT about how good Sista B'Nice sang today. It's NOT even about how the sermon made you feel. And open your ears for this one, it's also NOT about how many members 'your' church has. What church growth is about is simple: THE KINGDOM OF GOD.

27

If you haven't received this message deep down in your heart yet, then maybe you are part of the reason for the treason. What am I talking about? I'll explain. If you are part of a clique in your church that makes it a point NOT to welcome new people, to help them become new members, then you're part of the reason for the treason. What treason? Pushing people away instead of welcoming them into God's House. If you're not part of the growth in God's Kingdom, you're part of the gang that's trying to prevent it.

Growth in a "God" Church should be purposed. Members should be focused on helping those who are lost, 'find' their way into a relationship with God through His son Jesus Christ.

So many church members have become confused and conflicted about what their role in the church actually is. God did not save you for you! He saved you to serve. If you heart isn't serving it is selfish. And you cannot be useful to God without a heart for Him and His people. "But I'm the Head of so-and-so and so-and-so!" To that I say, "SO WHAT!"

28

In order to be a leader of anything, you must first learn how to be a follower of One thing. That One thing is not yourself, it is Christ. Once you learn how to follow the man God placed over you. Once you learn how to follow the man God made watchman over your soul. Once you learn how to follow without grumbling. Once you learn how to follow orders instead of always wanting to give them, THEN, you will be ready to grow and help the church do the same. Read my book, *Lord How Am I Doing*. It can help you identify areas of your church input and ministry impact, if any.

Many church members get stuck in the pews, constantly and comfortably learning the same things over and over and over, year after year without ever putting the learning to use, by putting their faith into action. If this is you...you need a growth check-up.

Again, church growth is mandatory. If churches don't grow in membership, or maturity, over a time period, it is my sincere belief that something is terribly wrong.

GROWTH IN CHURCH MEMBERS & MATURITY IS MANDATORY

Can you name or identify three things that shows your church is Growing, and three areas where it may not be growing?

29

My Church is Growing because?

1. _____

2. _____

3. _____

My Church may not be Growing because?

1. _____

2. _____

3. _____

BELIEVING

A "God" Church Must Be Believing. James 1:6 says that "when you ask God for anything, you must believe and not doubt..." Faith (**belief**) is the essence of things hoped for, the evidence of things not seen. Faith has the power to change us, recharge us, stir up the gift God placed in us; unlock the potential God created in us, so we can accomplish His will and His purpose for us! To do any of this requires that we walk by faith and not by sight. Are you a member of a church that believes everything in God's Word? Or one that dissects it for its own use and tries to ignore the rest? Proverbs 30:5 says "every word of God is pure" there's no need to add anything to it, or remove anything from it. But in order for it to make any sense to us, we must first **believe** it.

30

A "God" church helps its members see their purpose and believe their potential. **Faith has the power to release our potential in order to fulfill God's purpose**! What potential has God already placed in you that you don't believe because you focus on what you see and what others say?

• People **saw** Moses as a murderer, God **believed** in him as a deliverer.

•·People **saw** David as a boy, God **believed** in him as a giant killer.

•·People **saw** Saul the persecutor, Jesus **believed** in Paul as an apostle.

A "God" church teaches members to ignore what they see, and act on what they believe? A "God" church doesn't think, act, or react on doubt, it walks by Faith.

BELIEF WITHOUT ACTION, IS FAITH WITHOUT WORKS

Can you name or identify three things that shows your church is Believing, and three areas where it may not be believing?

31

My Church is Believing because?

1. _____

2. _____

3. _____

My Church may not be Believing because?

1. _____

2. _____

3. _____

PRAYING

A "God" Church must be a praying church. I don't mean just praying during the worship service on Sunday, I mean getting together to pray for the deliverance healing and growth of people. But, this process starts with the honesty of the people. A "Godly" church should teach that members should confess their sins so they can be healed. James 5:16 says this. But in 5:13-14 it says, "if anyone is in trouble, he should pray. If anyone is sick, the elders should pray over him and anoint him with oil in the name of the Lord."

32

It is my sincere belief that if a righteous man or woman "concentrates" their prayers on the specific issues that people are going through, it is powerful and effective (5:16).

For example, at the church I attended for twelve years, when the Pastor (whom I consider a righteous man) prays for the specific issues of people such as brother so-and-so needs deliverance from alcohol, or when sister so-and-so needed to be delivered from drug addiction, I've witnessed that deliverance. But it only came when the people confessed their sins to one another.

At the church I currently attend, almost every member has a prayer partner, and the growth that I see evident in the lives of the members is far reaching.

The commitment of the people to come together in the early morning, or wee hours of the night is and has been super effective. And is evident in many ways.

A CONCENTRATED PRAYER IS KEY TO GETTING THROUGH

Can you name or identify three things that shows your church is a Praying church, and three areas where it may not be Praying?

33

My Church is a Praying church because?

1. _____

2. _____

3. _____

My Church may not be Praying because?

1. _____

2. _____

3. _____

FASTING

A "God" Church must be a fasting church. Fasting in God's eyes is a sacrifice we make to show God that we are willing to suffer for a while in order to receive something we've asked Him to do. Each time fasting is referenced in the Bible, it is done after someone has asked God to do something. Most times of fasting led to entire villages such as Ninevah being delivered (book of Jonah). Not only did one person fast, but the entire village or town, fasted so God would hear their prayers, have compassion and work a miracle. If your church is not a church that teaches fasting, and doesn't fast about specific issues that need miracles from God, it should be.

For the past several years, my fasting schedule has been such that I commit myself to giving God back 10% of the days He allows me to live each month. This is where I start. On average, there are 30 days in a month. That means 10% of that, or 3 days, I fast. This is my general fast. And I schedule it on the 10th, 20th, and 30th of each month.

In addition to this fast, if our church, through the Pastor, calls for a fast, I pray about joining the effort, and if God leads me into this congregational fast, I'm obedient. There are other times that my wife and I may see a need to fast about our family or others.

34

I truly cannot measure the blessings that fasting is in my life and our lives. See my book, *Transform Your Schedule Transform Your Life* to learn more about the benefits of fasting.

FASTING IS SACRIFICE THAT MEANS MORE THAN NOT EATING

Can you name or identify three things that shows your church is a Fasting church, and three areas where it may not be Fasting?

35

My Church is a Fasting church because?

1. _____

2. _____

3. _____

My Church may not be Fasting because?

1. _____

2. _____

3. _____

◤ PRAISING

A "God" Church Must Be a Praising Church. Praise is an inward sign of our love for God manifested on the outside. It shows in the raising of our arms, clapping our hands, the bowing of our head, lying on the floor, crying out to God, speaking in tongues, jumping up and down, running the aisles, and giving God glory through words, song, music, or any of a variety of ways that shows God how much we love Him. God is worthy to be praised just because He is God and your church should actively praise Him at all times.

36

The Bible says that if we don't praise Him, the rocks will cry out.

"Godly" churches make no excuse for praising God. They just do it. There is no schedule to it, no order for it, no way to control it. It's something that happens in the spirit and comes out in signs evident to those around us that it's what we're doing. Praise can even be silent, shown through the very tears that run down your face.

Your praise to God should be personal, but should not in any way be stiffled, muffled, or stagnated by your church. Churches and the people in them, OWE GOD PRAISE. He is worthy, and way beyond deserving of it, just for saving our individual lives.

Your praise should be personal, but also passionate, and purposed. It should give God glory for all HE has done for us in, to, and through our lives.

PRAISING GOD CAN & SHOULD BE SHOWN IN MANY WAYS

Can you name or identify three things that shows your church is a Praising church, and three areas where it may not be Praising?

37

My Church is a Praising church because?

1. _____

2. _____

3. _____

My Church may not be Praising because?

1. _____

2. _____

3. _____

WORSHIPING

A "God" Church Must Be a Worshiping Church. Worship is a requirement for salvation. "True worship" takes place in spirit and in truth. Worship takes place by offering ourselves to God as living sacrifices that He can use for His purpose. Worship doesn't just take place during church services. "God" churches should be teaching people how to worship. Worship should happen when you get up in the morning. It should happen all during the day around whatever you're doing. It should happen before you lay down to go to sleep at night.

38

Everyone worships something. Whatever you spend most of your time doing, whatever your most focused on or trying to accomplish, is most likely what you worship. Whatever you spend most of your money on, is another sign of something you may be worshipping.

Again, "True worship" takes place in spirit and in truth. This means that you stop thinking or worrying about what others may see or say when you worship God (spirit). And, no matter what the consequences are, or who it offends, hurts, or exposes, you give God worship by always telling the (truth).

The highest form of worship is "obedience." But in order to be an obedient servant, you must first know who it is you are obeying. Jesus said if we Love Him we would "keep" His commandments. This is the ultimate sign that we are truly obedient.

WORSHIP IS SACRI-FICING OURSELVES TO BE USED BY GOD.

Can you name or identify three things that shows your church is a Worshiping church, and three areas where it may not be?

39

My Church is a Worshiping church because?

1. _____

2. _____

3. _____

My Church may not be Worshiping because?

1. _____

2. _____

3. _____

◤ HONORING

A "God" Church Must Honor God. This entire book is about ways a Godly church honors God. But there are three essential ways that we recognize a church that honors God.

(1) Honor God Through Tithing - based on the principles taught in Acts 5, and the reasons taught in Malachi 3, God's people give the first 10% of our income to support the church and the work of the ministry. Just like your rent or mortgage needs to be paid at your own house, the same needs to happen in God's house. Just like your light bill, gas bill, water bill, needs to be paid at your own house...so does the light bill, gas bill, water bill at the church. But how does your church honor God? Is it only through the efforts of its members? Or, does it set aside 10% of its income to honor God with a Tithe as a church? This 10% can be used as a way to help members in need, which certainly is a way to honor God.

(2) Honor God With Your Talent - If you've ever read my testimony, you'd know it shows that during my 15 years in leadership positions at two churches I attended, I used my God given gifts to help build up and edify the church in many areas. What are you doing with your gifts? A "God" church should be helping you recognize your gifts, and then show you how you can best use them in your church and in ministry.

(3) Honor God With Your Time - A "God" church helps members do something to honor God "after the benediction." It teaches members how & where to do ministry work during the week.

HONOR GOD WITH EVERY ELEMENT OF YOURSELF

Can you name or identify three things that shows your church is an Honoring church, and three areas where it may not be?

41

My Church is an Honoring church because?

1. _____

2. _____

3. _____

My Church may not be Honoring God because?

1. _____

2. _____

3. _____

Growing
Believing
Praying
Fasting
Praising
Worshiping
Honoring

42

Chapter Two
Did You Learn Anything?
Share Your Revelations At
Blog.LessonsForLifeBooks.com

CHAPTER

three

LOVING

A "God" Church Must Be Loving. Many people determine whether a church is a "God" church by how many older people are in the pews. Don't use this scale. All elders do not have love in their hearts. God is love (1st John 4:8). Love will only arrive at the church when those who have it bring it, walk in it, and show it in their actions. Being in Church doesn't make you a Christian any more than being in a garage makes you a car. Christians must show they are, by expressing love through action.

Love One Another as I have loved you. In John 13:34 this is what Jesus says is how we prove that we are His disciples. It is also echoed in Matthew 5:44. Jesus said love your enemies. Loving one another unconditionally is not easy. It starts with true forgiveness. True forgiveness is treating someone that has harmed you as if it never happened. This is exactly how God treats us. Even though we constantly mistreat God, Romans 5:8 says that "God demonstrates His own love for us in this: While we were still sinners, Christ died for us." **Love One Another** is one of two new commandments that sums up all the law and the prophets (John 13:34). If you were having problems and wandered away from the church, does the Pastor or other members love you enough to come out of the comfort of the church walls to try and find you? If they do, this is a very good indication of a "God" church.

Matthew 18:12-14 says that if a Shepherd has a hundred sheep and one of them wanders away, he leaves the ninety-nine, just to go find the one that is lost.

A LOVING CHURCH IS A FORGIVING CHURCH

Can you name or identify three things that shows your church is a Loving church, and three areas where it may not be?

45

My Church is a Loving church because?

1. _____

2. _____

3. _____

My Church may not be Loving because?

1. _____

2. _____

3. _____

NURTURING

A "God" Church Must Be Nurturing. This does not come easy. The leadership in churches are supposed to be "as nurturing as mothers caring for their children" (1st Thessalonians 2:7). The process does not happen overnight. Church Leadership should nurture its:

- *Long-time members into ministry.*
- *New members into growth from infants to adults.*
- *Weak Christians into strong ones.*

46

New members are like baby chicks following behind its adult mother. The mother cares for them, feeds them, protects them, watches out for them, teaches them, trains them, supports them. When they are grown, trusts them to make the right decisions on behalf of the church and in their own ministries. Churches should be focused on **nurturing** its members for growth to support the existing church and ministry and to work in their own ministries. It should hold regular classes and workshops to teach members about every aspect of church conception, its history, its growth, its role and responsibilities to the community, etc. If this isn't happening (and you aren't helping to start it), it should be. Churches should be **nurturing** in their own communities. IF a church is not active in its own community, it should be. The church is the strong tower of every community. It is supposed to be the leader and representative for everything that is right within the community.

If your church isn't active in outreach, by fellowshiping and helping to meet the needs of the people within its community, it should be. But also remember, it may take "you" to make it happen.

NURTURING IS A PROCESS THAT PRODUCES MATURITY

Can you name or identify three things that shows your church is a Nurturing church, and three areas where it may not be?

47

My Church is a Nurturing church because?

1. _____

2. _____

3. _____

My Church may not be Nurturing because?

1. _____

2. _____

3. _____

AGREEING

A "God" Church Must Be On One Accord. I had an experience once where I had to correct a man who was teaching another person that the Bible was man's interpretation of God Word. I had to tell him that I did not **agree** and that those who wrote books in the Bible were "witnesses" to events that happened during those times. The Bible, therefore, is a history book, written by men who were directly inspired by God to write things down for future generations as examples of how to live and how not to live. I backed up my point from 1st Corinthians 10:11.

48

A "God" church must teach is members the raw truth about the Bible so that everyone can be on one accord. If one person believes one thing about the Bible, and another believes something else, it causes confusion. The man I corrected had been in church most of his life. His core knowledge came from a church. In Matthew 18:20 says, "For where two or three come together in my Name, there I am with them." A "God" church teaches its members that God is God, and Jesus Christ is God's Son who died on the cross for our sins, was raised from the dead and now sits at the right hand of the Father. And that the Holy Spirit was sent back by Jesus when He returned to Heaven in order to guide us into all truth. If your church doesn't agree with, doesn't teach or doesn't promote these truths, it is probably not a "God" church.

God's spirit resides in truth. He cannot lie. Therefore, anything contrary to what God said about Himself, His Son, and/or His Spirit, is not of God.

WHEN TWO OR MORE IN HIS WILL AGREE, CHANGE HAPPENS

Can you name or identify three things that shows your church is in Agreement with God's will, three areas where it may not be?

49

My Church is in Agreement because?

1. _____

2. _____

3. _____

My Church may not be in Agreement because?

1. _____

2. _____

3. _____

FORGIVING

A "God" Church Must Be Forgiving. Members backslide. Proverbs 24:16. Members will sin. That's a given. They may sin against other members, and may even sin against the church. But, if your church and its members does not take the stand to forgive them, and put them right back on track, it should be. Proverbs 19:11 says "it is to a man's glory to overlook an offense."

50

Forgiving someone who has sinned against you as if it never happened is God's way. Jesus put it this way, "For if you forgive men when they sin against you, your heavenly Father will also forgive you. But if you do not forgive men their sins, your Father will not forgive your sins" (Matthew 6:14-15).

Forgiving the act and the person is how forgiveness works. We must forgive the sin and the sinner. This is how God treats us. Isaiah 43:25 says, "I, even I, and He who blots our your transgressions for my own sake, and remembers your sins no more."

If you've ever heard the saying "forgive and forget" Isaiah 43:25 is where it comes from. It's how God treats our sin. And we should do the same to others. The greatest benefit of forgiveness is giving glory to God. But, the added bonus is that true forgiveness restores relationships.

Satan does not value relationships, nor does he like forgiveness. He comes to steal, kill and destroy both. But the moment you forgive the sin and the sinner, you've just gotten the victory!

A FORGIVING CHURCH RESTORES RELATIONSHIPS

Can you name or identify three things that shows your church is in a Forgiving church, and three areas where it may not be?

51

My Church is a Forgiving church because?

1. _____

2. _____

3. _____

My Church may not be a Forgiving church because?

1. _____

2. _____

3. _____

◤ COMPASSIONATE

A "God" Church must be compassionate. In Matthew 14:13-21, Jesus showed compassion on the people by healing the sick (verse 14). Then, as evening approached the disciples were going to send the people away to "purchase" their own food; Jesus said to them, "you feed them." The disciples objected to the notion by saying it would take lots of money to do so. Jesus wasn't trying to show the disciples that He had power to feed that many, but the lesson was so the disciples would learn they should have a heart of compassion to do so, regardless of the cost.

52

A "Godly" Church shows compassion in a variety of ways. For example, using a percentage of the church's income to help members in crisis is a really important way. If your church doesn't do this, beware. Acts 2:45 shows us this concept. Keeping up with you and your family is another way churches show compassion. If this does not happen, it should. There are some churches that are lacking in their relationship with members and their approach toward helping members. That is not Biblical. It is selfish. Being **compassionate** comes from the heart of people. If it doesn't exist already, don't just expect it to happen. Sometimes "you" have to be the one to make it happen or show others that it should. While some already have compassion, it takes years for others. Here's an example: there are people on our streets holding up signs. Very few ask for money, we just assume they do.

If we apply James 2:14-17 or Matthew 14:16, I believe more Christians would show compassion by not only feeding them physically, but spiritually, by handing them tracts, Bibles, etc.

COMPASSION STARTS IN THE SPIRIT & OUT VIA THE HEART

Can you name or identify three things that shows your church is a Compassionate church, and three areas where it may not be?

53

My Church is a Compassionate church because?

1. _____

2. _____

3. _____

My Church may not be a Compassionate church because?

1. _____

2. _____

3. _____

54

Loving	
Nurturing	Chapter Three
Agreeing	Did You Learn Anything?
Forgiving	Share Your Revelations At
Compassionate	Blog.LessonsForLifeBooks.com

CHAPTER

four

ACCEPTING

A "God" Church Must Be Accepting Of Others. I've seen many instances where people who were not members of the church who had different circumstances (homeless, ex-cons, etc.) were treated differently than those who are already part of the church. In Matthew 9:12-13, Jesus says, "It is not the healthy who need a doctor, but the sick. But go and learn what this means...For I have not come to call the righteous, but sinners."

Being Accepting of Others comes through knowing that the church is a hospital for those who are spiritually sick. When people who are spiritually sick check into the emergency room called the church, if the members who used to be patients themselves, and those who still are, even after decades of being there, treat those who are just coming in differently, it shouldn't be this way.

Being Accepting of Others comes through having a heart of compassion; having a heart that doesn't judge others; having a heart for helping to meet the needs of others, both spiritually and physically. Jesus spoke about this in many instances. He spoke about accepting others in Luke 14:12-14 when He taught us that when we give lunches or dinners or parties or celebrations, invite the poor, the crippled, the lame, the blind, and we will be blessed. Because if we only invite our friends, church members, relatives

56

or rich neighbors, once they give an event and invite you, you are repaid. But because those in need cannot repay you, you will be repaid when Jesus returns.

THE CHURCH SHOULD ACCEPT ALL WHO ARE SPIRITUALLY SICK

Can you name or identify three things that shows your church is in an Accepting church, and three areas where it may not be?

My Church is an Accepting church because?

1. _____

2. _____

3. _____

My Church may not be an Accepting church because?

1. _____

2. _____

3. _____

◤ HEALING

A "God" Church Must Be Healing. Again, the church is a hospital for the spiritually sick. And it must be actively involved in working to heal its members through the examples Jesus showed when He was here. Every time Jesus healed someone, He asked them if they "believed" they could be healed. Or, He said to them, "your faith has made you whole."

58

Doctors existed in the days Jesus was here. The woman who had an issue of blood for 12 years, had been to many doctors to try and get well. But ultimately, it was her spirit that released the faith she needed to seek Christ with all her heart, in order to **heal**.

In my book, *Disease Carrier, Don't Be A Host For Sin* I point out that if more churches focused on identifying and exposing sin in the lives of its members, **healing** would take place. James 5:14 says, "If any one of you is sick, call the elders of the church to pray over him and anoint him with oil in the Name of the Lord. And the prayer offered "in faith" will make the sick person well. If he has sinned, he will be forgiven.

Therefore, confess your sins to each other and pray for each other so that you may be **healed**. The prayer of a righteous man is powerful and effective.

God is not moved by need. Everyone has needs. God is moved by faith. Miracles of healing happen in our lives when we have the faith to manifest them.

HEALING TAKE PLACE WHEN FAITH HAPPENS

Can you name or identify three things that shows your church is in a Healing church, and three areas where it may not be?

My Church is a Healing church because?

1. _____

2. _____

3. _____

My Church may not be a Healing church because?

1. _____

2. _____

3. _____

59

ADAPTING

A "God" Church Must Be Able To Adapt. This is of paramount importance because the society we live in is constantly changing but our mission as Christians remains the same. Churches must adapt to societal changes. Many churches still hang on to traditions just because the church has done it a certain way for decades. Such traditions as opening the doors on Sunday and waiting for people to come to you. That's not the way Jesus, the Disciples, or the Apostles did it in the Bible, and that is not the way we should be doing it today.

60

In order to **adapt** to changing times and a changing society churches should be open to the fact that there are more nationalities and cultures living in our communities than ever before. How do we reach those individuals? **By offering services and programs that meet their needs**. For example, if your community has an influx of Hispanic people living there now, on one Sunday each month, your church could invite a Hispanic pastor and worship team in to host the service. This is outreach that is **adapting** to changing times. The great commission gave us the command to go into all the world to preach, teach and make disciples of all nations. So, how do we reach people in other cultures and languages with the Gospel of Jesus Christ, if your church isn't willing to **adapt**? Does your church expect them to remain lost, with no hope of salvation?

How does your church reach the lost in other cultures? Wait for someone who can speak their language to join your church? It may never happen. A "God" church must be wiling to adapt.

CHURCHES REACH MORE LOST SOULS BY ADAPTING

Can you name or identify three things that shows your church is an Adapting church, and three areas where it may not be?

61

My Church is Adapting because?

1. _____

2. _____

3. _____

My Church may not be Adapting because?

1. _____

2. _____

3. _____

HELPING

A "God" Church Must Be Helping. This does not come easy. The leadership in many churches believe that members are supposed to help the church through tithes and offerings but that the church is not supposed to help the members when they get in a bind. I know several situations where the leadership in churches deny the requests of members who need help by saying the money isn't supposed to be used that way. That's not Biblical, it's selfish.

I don't advocate churches to open their purse strings to members who have been on the roll less than a year. Otherwise, you may get people to join church looking for a handout instead of looking for Jesus. I also don't advocate making a habit of helping the same people over and over and over again. Otherwise, they'll just spend their income on things other than necessities and start relying and depending on the church to bail them out. However, if you have been a member of a church paying tithes and giving offerings for two, three, five, ten years, and you get in a financial bind, but your church tells you you're on your own, it shouldn't be that way. It's not Biblical, it's selfish. First, pray. Ask God to touch the heart of the leadership to see that **helping** people, especially faithful members, is God's way. Read 2nd Cor. 9:6-15. How do churches Tithe? I believe churches should set aside 10% ten percent of it's income as Tithe to support members in dire need and to be **helpful** in some capacity.

62

I firmly believe that if a church not only takes care of its members spiritually, but also helps meet their emergency needs periodically, churches would have and keep more members.

A "GOD" CHURCH HELP MEMBERS WHO ARE IN NEED

Can you name or identify three things that shows your church is a Helping church, and three areas where it may not be?

63

My Church is a Helping church because?

1. _____

2. _____

3. _____

My Church may not be a Helping church because?

1. _____

2. _____

3. _____

PARTICIPATING

A "God" Church must be participating in ministry "after the benediction." Many churches exist just to have church. I know many churches that schedule one program after another after another just to raise money to keep the doors open. There is no active ministry outside the church; no outreach or involvement or effort to reach the lost in the community, no fellowship within the community; and no effort to take strongholds the devil has set up in the community (such as dope houses), to destroy them and establish God's Kingdom in the community. These things can only happen if the members are taught they need to happen, and if the people have it in their hearts to make it happen. What should happen **"after the benediction?"** After Jesus preached and taught, He fed the hungry, visited the sick, ministered to prisoners, took time for widows and orphans; and that's exactly what He told us to do (Matthew 25:35-36). This is real ministry work. The world calls it social service and are getting paid to do what Christians should be doing freely. If your church is not **participating** in the ministry that Jesus started, it should be. Scripture says, Faith (Church) without Works (Ministry) is dead. Here's an example of a God church and its ministry schedule:

SUNDAY	Sunday school and church (worship, praise, prayer and hearing God's Word)
MONDAY	Reach the lost by handing out booklets and tracks everywhere you go.
TUESDAY	Visit the sick in hospitals, nursing homes, etc. (read, pray and sing to them).
WEDNESDAY	Attend Bible Study to continue your growth in the wisdom of God's Word.
THURSDAY	Feed the hungry and hand out booklets and tracks to them.
FRIDAY	Minister to prisoners (write letters and deliver booklets and tracts).
SATURDAY	Rest, fast, pray and study God's Word alone and/or with family.

64

Again, Faith (Church) without Works (Ministry) is dead. If you need more information on this vital subject, read my book titled: *"Church On Sunday, Nothing On Monday"*.

BEWARE OF CHURCH ON SUNDAY, NOTHING ON MONDAY

Can you name or identify three things that shows your church is a Participating church, and three areas where it may not be?

65

My Church Participates in the Ministry Jesus started because?

1. _____

2. _____

3. _____

My Church may not be Participating because?

1. _____

2. _____

3. _____

66

Accepting Healing Adapting Helping Participating	Chapter Four Did You Learn Anything? Share Your Revelations At Blog.LessonsForLifeBooks.com

C H A P T E R

five

UNDERSTANDING

A "God" Church Must Be Understanding. How does your church deal with sin in the new members? How does it handle sin issues in the members who've been there a long time? How about sin in the church officers? How does it react to sin if it occurs in someone on the pastoral staff? Is it understanding?

Sin happens to all of us. All have sinned and fallen short of the glory of God. God understands that we are sinners. So much so, that He "blots out all our transgressions and for His own sake, remembers them no more" (Isaiah 43:25). A "God" church follows this example. It understands member's weaknesses, and treats them as God does, not holding it over them, judging them, or reminding them about it every chance they get. And, in most cases, it also does not prevent them from continuing to serve as officers if they fall short. The Bible says for though a righteous man falls seven times, he rises again. It's expected that we will fall or commit sin at some point. How a church reacts to it determines its status, in my opinion, as a "God" church. God's thoughts are higher than our thoughts. His ways higher than our ways. "His understanding no one can fathom" (Isaiah 40:28). A "God" church follows, teaches and promotes Proverbs 3:5-6, which says "Trust in the Lord with all your heart and lean not unto your own understanding but in all our ways acknowledge Him and He will direct our paths." The understanding way God treats sin, so should we.

68

A "God" church doesn't need to analyze why sin happens in its members, it follows God's example by forgiving them, forgetting it, and moving forward to help members grow beyond it.

A CHURCH OF UNDER- STANDING SHOWS TRUE FORGIVENESS

Can you name or identify three things that shows your church is an Understanding church, and three areas where it may not be?

69

My Church is Understanding because?

1. _____

2. _____

3. _____

My Church may not be Understanding because?

1. _____

2. _____

3. _____

LISTENING

A "God" Church Must Be Good Listeners. In most churches I've been to, during times when people were in need and needed someone to either talk to, or some help in one way or another, they would almost always run into someone from the pastoral staff who only wanted to judge the situation and tell them what they think they should do on the surface and send them on their way; before they ever listened to root of the person's problem, and deal with the source of the stronghold.

James 1:19 says "everyone should be quick to **listen**, slow to speak and slow to become angry." Proverbs 18:13 says, "He who answers before **listening**, that is his folly and his shame." And, Proverbs 1:5 says, "Let the wise **listen** and add to their learning." Being a good **listener** requires patience. Romans 10:17 says faith comes by hearing, and hearing by the Word of God. In order to hear God's Word we must take time to **listen** in order to hear the message that God has for us.

I've been in many leadership meetings where I've seen evidence of the damage this microwave society has done to people's brains, where seemingly everyone is rushing to do this and rushing to do that, *going nowhere fast*, which has led to many leaders in the church not wanting to take time to listen, they just want to get their point, or opinion, or interpretation across.

If your church is not taking time to listen to the needs of its members, and members of its own community so it can take action and help them, it should be.

IF A CHURCH DOESN'T LISTEN IT WON'T HEAR

Can you name or identify three things that shows your church is a Listening church, and three areas where it may not be?

71

My Church is a Listening church because?

1. _____

2. _____

3. _____

My Church may not be Listening to its members because?

1. _____

2. _____

3. _____

TEACHING

A "God" Church Must Be A Teaching Church. I've seen many churches that only focus on teaching from man's interpretation of the Bible. This is wrong. Churches should just teach the Bible as it's written. The Bible is crystal clear in its parables, precepts, concepts, covenants and revelations. Romans 10:17 says "faith comes by hearing and hearing by the Word of God." It does not say faith comes by hearing the word of men.

72

A "God" Church Must Be A Teaching Church but it must be teaching the right things. In a church I attended 12 years, I finally heard my Pastor say that churches have been teaching things the wrong way for decades. I praised and thanked God for the Pastor's growth! An example of something that has been taught wrong for years in many pulpits across the world, is that *when we die we go straight to Heaven*. That is wrong. The Bible makes numerous references that we go "to sleep" and wait for judgement day along with everyone else.

I've seen many churches purchase Sunday School books and other curriculum written and based on man's interpretation. Make certain your church takes its Sunday School and Bible Study curriculum directly from the Bible. The Bible is already full of stories written to be taught to any and every age group. It doesn't need to be altered. In fact, in 2nd Corinthians 4:2 it says not to alter it.

Proverbs 30:5 says, God's word is already flawless, don't add to it or God will rebuke you and prove you a liar. Churches, especially in these last days, should be teaching the raw truth of the Bible.

A "GOD" CHURCH TEACHES FROM GOD'S WORD

Can you name or identify three things that shows your church is a Teaching church, and three areas where it may not be?

73

My Church Teaches the right things because?

1. _____

2. _____

3. _____

My Church may not be Teaching the right things because?

1. _____

2. _____

3. _____

TRAINING

A "God" Church must focus on training others for serving in the church, and for ministry work outside the church. And, should train its members about the distinct and vast difference between the two. To **train** members **for service in the church** the leaders and the laypersons (pastors, deacons, deaconesses, stewards, secretaries, ushers, choir members, musicians, etc.) should regularly take courses at the local, national and even the international level, that are applicable to their specific role in the church.

To **train** members **for ministry work outside the church**, the leadership needs to direct members to take courses applicable to their ministry focus. The courses should be designed to train workers how to be most effective. For example: a ministry of feeding the hungry has several aspects that most people are not aware of. There are food pantries, soup kitchens, acts of kindness on the street, and other things that should be taught to those willing to do the work. There is also a need for people who are gifted at recruiting the volunteers. There are rules and laws for storing and serving food that need to be adhered to. And, there are organizations already established that can provide assistance in the form of in-kind services that can benefit your church; and there are several types of grants available as well. Such **training**, in the specified area of ministry, is vital.

74

There is a constant need for ministry work **outside the church**, but few willing workers (Matthew 9:37), so it's vitally important that those who have been trained, take time to train others.

A "GOD" CHURCH TRAINS ITS MEMBERS TO WORK IN MINISTRY

Can you name or identify three things that shows your church is a Training church, and three areas where it may not be?

75

My Church is a Training church because?

1. _____

2. _____

3. _____

My Church may not be Training its members because?

1. _____

2. _____

3. _____

READING, HEARING & STUDYING

A "God" Church Must Read the Bible Into Your Hearing.
It is important because God's Word is living and active. Sharper than any double-edged sword, it penetrates even to dividing soul and spirit, joints and marrow; it judges the thoughts and attitudes of the heart (Hebrews 4:12). Reading God's Word into your hearing will start to transform even those who don't want to be. **Reading the Bible** into your hearing is important because all Scripture is God-breathed and is useful for teaching, rebuking, correcting, and training in righteousness, so that the man (and woman) of God may be thoroughly equipped for every good work (2nd Timothy 3:16-17). If you don't know the Word, how can you teach it, or rebuke someone with it; or correct anyone with it? God's Word is useful for training in righteousness, so if you want to be righteous, God's Word will teach you how to be.

Hearing the Bible read to you is important because FAITH comes by hearing and hearing by the Word of God (Romans 10:17). Your faith depends on hearing the Word of God. It starts the process of you calling on the name of the Lord (verse 13). It helps you believing in the One you call on (verse 14). And, it says you can't hear without a preacher. More importantly, don't just be a hearer of the Word, you must put your faith into action by doing what the Word says (James 1:22-25). **Studying the Bible** is important because 2nd Timothy 2:15 says study to show thyself approved unto God so you can be a worker who won't be ashamed

76

and are able to rightly divide (discern) the Word of truth. Ezra devoted himself to the study and observance of the Law of the Lord, and to teaching it to Israel (Ezra 7:10).

READ WITH EYES; HEAR WITH EARS; STUDY WITH HEART

Can you name or identify three things that shows your church is a Reading, Hearing and Studying church, and three areas where it may not be?

77

My Church is a Reading, Hearing and Studying church because?

1. _____

2. _____

3. _____

My Church may not be Reading, Hearing and Studying because?

1. _____

2. _____

3. _____

Understanding
Listening
Teaching
Training
Read/Hear/Study

Chapter Five
Did You Learn Anything?
Share Your Revelations At
Blog.LessonsForLifeBooks.com

CHAPTER

six

◤ CREATING

A "God" Church Must Be Creating Opportunities for Growth. Members of any church are only going to grow into maturity if the church leadership creates opportunities that incite, spur and mandate growth. For example, if your church never holds or participates in any training, workshops, or conferences, it should. It should be creating ministries that meet the needs of problems that didn't exist 2000 years ago. Opportunities for growth are created by church leaders who are taught and who understand how important this component is. Growth and maturity of a church is vitally important, as it says in the growth section of this book. In my book, *Church On Sunday, Nothing On Monday* I show the path for growth in most traditional churches. It reads this way:

80

Church
- New Member = Kindergarten
- Service in the Church = Elementary School
- Serving in the Church = Junior High
- Leadership in the Church = Senior High (graduation)

Ministry
- Serving Outside the Church = College
  - -- (Feeding the hungry)
  - -- (Visiting the sick)
  - -- (Helping strangers)
  - -- (Ministering to prisoners)
  - -- (Taking care of widows and orphans)

> There are many ministry areas needed today that didn't exist 2000 years ago. Such as teen pregnancy & drug counseling.

When churches do this their members grow to become useful in God's Kingdom in many areas.

A "God" church should create opportunities for its members to be trained to serve in the church, become the next leadership in the church, then graduate into serving outside the church in ministry.

CHURCHES THAT DON'T CREATE... STAGNATE

Can you name or identify three things that shows your church is Creating Opportunities for Growth and three areas where it may not be?

81

My Church is Creating Opportunities for growth because?

1. _____

2. _____

3. _____

My Church may not be Creating opportunities because?

1. _____

2. _____

3. _____

DEVELOPING

A "God" Church Must Develop Ministries That Impact.
I've seen many churches get stuck in the past. They don't create ministries that keep up with the times, or that impact society in a way that keeps them being the pillar of the community, the strong tower, the lamp that lights the way. They get stuck doing things the way they've done it for years, thereby standing in the way of their own growth. Churches need to be **developing** ministries that meet the needs of its members. For example, all churches have married couples but few develop a ministry that helps couples deal with the issues they face in their marriage; All churches have single individuals but few develop a ministry that teaches them how to be equally yoked with other believers; All churches have gifted people, but few develop a ministry that holds classes or training sessions that teaches people how to use their gifts. Many churches have members with drug and alcohol problems but few develop a ministry that teaches how to deal with addictions. Churches should be **developing** ministries that focus on establishing God's Kingdom in their own communities. It is my sincere belief that Churches should be masters at economic development and should own vacant land and other property in the community. This type of impact helps keep drug dealers from ever setting up shop on the block; helps church members establish housing in the community; helps establish sources of income for the church; and helps keep property from becoming blighted.

82

I also believe that churches should be **developing** or buying businesses in its own community; in order to further establish God's Kingdom in the community.

A "GOD" CHURCH DOES "GOD" IN THEIR COMMUNITY

Can you name or identify three things that shows your church is Developing Ministries that impact your community and three areas where it may not be?

83

My Church is Developing Impactful Ministries because?

1. _____

2. _____

3. _____

My Church may not be Developing Impactful Ministries because?

1. _____

2. _____

3. _____

BUILDING

A "God" Church Must Be Building Relationships With People in the Community. Very few churches I've been to know anything about its neighbors. They don't know their names, their children, relatives, their professions, or their skills. If your church is like the one I attended for 12 years, and another I attended for 3 years, the church always has a need for something. But when it is seeking to fill that need, it rarely if ever uses people right in its own community.

84

Here's an example: If your church needs training on how to **build** an economic development plan, or training on how to develop property to expand God's Kingdom and presence in the community, or training on how to **build** and manage a senior housing project, and you don't have those skills in a person or people within your church, how about finding a person that does this right in your own community? What better way to **build** lasting relationships with people in the community? And, maybe even gain new members from those same people.

A "God" church knows, says and promotes to its members how important it is to be **building** relationships with people in its own community. It is active in the neighborhood group, its hospital, its homeless shelter, its jails and prisons, its senior homes, and other places that are within its own community.

A "God" church is actively involved in building its members into strong, bold Christians that are useful in service to God both in church and in ministry, RIGHT IN ITS OWN COMMUNITY!

A "GOD" CHURCH HAS RELATIONSHIPS IN ITS OWN COMMUNITY

Can you name or identify three things that shows your church is Building Relationships that impact your community and three areas where it may not be?

85

My Church is Building Community Relationships because?

1. _____

2. _____

3. _____

My Church may not be Building Community Relations because?

1. _____

2. _____

3. _____

INVOLVING

A "God" Church Must Involve The Entire Congregation in Church and in Ministry. There are several gifted people in your church. But if you never ask them what area(s) they are gifted in, how will you know?

A "God" church surveys members from time to time (annually) to get a list of the skills they have or, if they have a learned a new skill that can be used in the church on in ministry?

A "God" church must **involve** the entire congregation in the worship, the work and the growth of the church and the ministry.

86

A "God" church has a strong new member focus, and a strong youth focus, because without either of these groups, every church will eventually cease to operate. In my book, *Welcome To Our Church: Guide For Creating New Member Packets* I outline several things a "God" church should do to ensure that their new members are a priority. Youth should receive the same attention.

A "God" church **involves** all its members in church and ministry because if no one is ever trained to take over a task that someone else is currently doing, how will that task continue? Jesus chose twelve to continue His work, and those twelve trained groups of others, then there were 72, etc.

If churches rely on one person to lead an area, without ever training someone else in the same area so the work continues, it prevents both the leader and other members from growing.

INVOLVING OTHER MEMBERS ENSURES THE WORK CONTINUES

Can you name or identify three things that shows your church is regularly Involving members in the church and ministry and three areas where it may not be?

87

My Church is constantly Involving other members because?

1. _____

2. _____

3. _____

My Church may not be Involving other members because?

1. _____

2. _____

3. _____

REACHING

A "God" Church Must Be Reaching Out. The church was founded by Jesus Christ. He gave the great commission to go into all the world to teach and preach the Gospel and to make disciples of all nations. Baptizing them in the name of Jesus. Churches must reach out with this message, first to those right in its own community, then to their city, their state, their country, and on to the rest of the world, using the technology that enables it.

A "God" church follows the examples Jesus set by traveling from place to place to ensure that the Good News of the Gospel was preached and taught everywhere and that it would continue long after He returned to Heaven.

88

There are constantly people moving into and your community. A "God" church gets updated mailing lists regularly, sends postcards, introducing themselves, letting neighbors know what services, and resources, and programs, and ministries are available, and also taking time to personally welcome them to the neighborhood.

A "God" church is one that does not just open the doors of the church waiting for people to come to you. It reaches its arms out into the community and to the world the way Jesus did. After all, God reached His arms way down here from Heaven in the form of His Son Jesus Christ.

He sacrificed His only son to ensure that we could have the opportunity to grab hold of salvation, and walk with Him, hand in hand, while He reached out to neighbors.

REACHING OUT REQUIRES US TO REACH FROM WITHIN

Can you name or identify three things that shows your church is Reaching Out and three areas where it may not be?

89

My Church is constantly Reaching Out because?

1. _____

2. _____

3. _____

My Church may not be Reaching Out because?

1. _____

2. _____

3. _____

90

Creating
Developing
Involving
Building
Reaching

Chapter Six
Did You Learn Anything?
Share Your Revelations At
Blog.LessonsForLifeBooks.com

CHAPTER

seven

UNVEILING

A "God" Church Should Help Remove the Veil. This happens by helping others come out of darkness and from being blinded by satan, so they can see the truth about Jesus (2nd Corinthians 3:12-16). If this isn't an active part of the church, it should be.

Darkness does two primary things:

1. Masquerades as light.

2. Establishes a stronghold in your life.

92

The role of the church is to help you see the truth by **unveiling** the tricks of the enemy through exposure, so you can recognize his schemes, and be delivered from them.

Jesus showed us the example of how to expose sin, call it out, name it, and confront it, so it will help the person affected by it, and serve as a warning to others so they won't fall for or in it.

Ephesians 4:18 says, having their understanding darkened, being alienated from the life of God through the ignorance that is in them, because of the blindness of their heart.

And, Ephesians 5:8-14 provides a summary to this subject by exposing the darkness to light so the truth can be revealed.

2nd Corinthians 3:14-16 says that until a person comes to Christ, their mind is blinded by the veil, which covers their understanding of who Christ is.

A "GOD" CHURCH RE-MOVES THE VEIL FROM MEMBER'S MINDS

Can you name or identify three things that shows your church is Removing the Veil and three areas where it may not be?

93

My Church is Removing the Veil because?

1. _____

2. _____

3. _____

My Church may not be Removing the Veil because?

1. _____

2. _____

3. _____

WINNING

A "God" Church is Focused On Winning Souls. "He who wins souls is wise" (Proverbs 11:30). Churches win souls by making it a top priority to help people receive the free gift of salvation by:

1. Offering them Jesus Christ as their Lord and Savior.

2. Baptizing them with water in the Name of Jesus.

3. Helping them to receive the Holy Spirit.

This is the complete process of salvation. You cannot have one or two, you must have all three. It is identified in Acts 2:38, and referenced in many other places in the Bible.

94

Winning souls for God through Jesus Christ takes work. But the labor and yoke is easy and burden is light if you are ready to offer yourself as a living sacrifice to be used as a willing vessel.

God can take your "willing" and put it with His "able" to make miraculous things happen for you and for others through you.

Whether you are a small or large church, the reality that some of your members may not make it to Heaven should be alarming, but also serve as an alarm that we, as chosen laborers on this field of battle, still have much work to do. It is our duty, now that we are saved, to help lead others to salvation. We were saved, to serve. And our assignment is simple: Fulfill the Great Commission.

If your church isn't growing in membership or in maturity, this may be the reason. Winning souls should be the main focus of every church, and if it isn't, you need to re-examine your mission.

A "GOD" CHURCH MAKES WINNING SOULS ITS TOP PRIORITY

Can you name or identify three things that shows your church is Winning Souls and three areas where it may not be?

95

My Church is Winning Souls because?

1. _____

2. _____

3. _____

My Church may not be Winning Souls because?

1. _____

2. _____

3. _____

96

Unveiling
Winning

Chapter Seven
Did You Learn Anything?
Share Your Revelations At
Blog.LessonsForLifeBooks.com

CHAPTER

epilogue

EPILOGUE

I wrote this book to help those who are looking for a "God" church, know what to look for in your search to find one.

I need to let you know and you need to be aware that not everyone's church home process is the same. Let the Holy Spirit guide you to the place you need to be.

If you're totally and completely new to church, and have no idea what I just said, or what the Holy Spirit is, let me explain it this way: there is or has been or will be an urging, deep down within the very core of your being, that will let you know when you have been led to, or are in the right place.

If you are in a church and know beyond the shadow of any doubt that it is not the right one for you, if you spend years wondering whether or not you should leave, then you're not following God's lead, but rather may be stuck there because of the relationships with the people. God can and will use you anywhere, but He wants you to go where He has sent you.

On any of the pages of this book, if you wrote in anything in the bottom section for "My Church may not be...because" ask yourself if you're the one helping to create this problem, or if you can be one of the ones to help solve it.

98

The world is abnormal. It is out of the natural order that God created for things to exist. Being Christian is what helps us become normal.

Remember:
If you're not part
of the problem,
you are or can be,
part of the solution.

99

TRINITY RECOGNITION

A "God" Church Must Recognize the Trinity. This is vitally important. A church should give honor to God, His Son Jesus Christ, and the Holy Spirit. Many people in the world will probably argue that the word "trinity" is never used in the Bible. Just remember what 2nd Corinthians 4:4 says, "the god of this age (satan) has blinded the minds of unbelievers, so that they cannot see the light of the gospel of Jesus Christ, who is the image of God."

Trinity Recognition in a church should recognize and promote Ephesians 4:5, which says, "One Lord, One Faith, One Baptism."

100

Trinity Recognition in a church should remind it's members from time to time that Jesus said, "anyone who does not believe in Me, does not have the Father." **Trinity Recognition** in a church should help you be aware of the fact that as a male, you are or can be someone's father, someone's son, and have God's spirit. As a female, you are or can be a mother, someone's daughter, and have God's spirit. **Trinity Recognition** in a church makes you aware of the fact that that God, Jesus and the Holy Spirit are called many things in the Bbile and this should not surprise you. Think about your own life. Have you ever been a provider? A comforter? A healer? A carpenter? A friend to the friendless? A present help in times of trouble? How many other descriptions could you add to this list?

May God Bless your journey.

Thank You

I've written over 80 books to date. This Ministry is an immeasurable Blessing in my life, and I'm grateful to God for His redemption, reuse, restoration, and reclamation, as my life many years before this was nothing more than a reckless shell of a man.

I'm including this note of thanks to all the readers of this book, because in these last days, establishing a relationship with God through His Son, Jesus Christ, is critical. And the protocol that Jesus established is to come through the doors of the church. He is coming back to harvest the church. That means if you are not a part of the Body of Christ, you need to be. Your family needs to be. Your friends, relatives, co-workers, and everyone else you know needs to be.

I'm also including a note of thanks for those who are tasked with helping your pastor, priest, bishop, etc., make your church a God church. It will not happen overnight, and it may take years to get there, but know that you CAN get there. I thank you because without you allowing your gifts, skills, talents, abilities, memory, knowledge, resources, and willingness to used in this process, it may never get done. Lastly, if you ever need assistance in making this process happen in your church, feel free to email me. Go to the Contact Page on the website: LessonsForLifeBooks.com

...it will eventually make it to my desk.

Contact

Author: Keith Hammond
President
Lessons For Life Books, Inc.
7455 France Avenue South #305
Edina, MN 55435

(952) 884-5498 ofc
(952) 884-3785 fax

author@LessonsForLifeBooks.com

web: LessonsForLifeBooks.com

How to Find Us:

Google:
'keith hammond lessons for life books'

Barnes & Noble:
bn.com
'keith hammond'

Bookwire.com
'keith hammond'

Amazon:
'keith hammond' plus 'book title'

Kindle:
'keith hammond' plus 'book title'

103

Catalog Reminder:
The best way to get an overall view of the more than 80 books I've written, is to download the full-color, interactive catalog from our website.

LessonsForLifeBooks.com/catalog.html

Every book page has a link to the preview of that book, and includes ISBN info, ordering info, etc.

GOD CHURCHES ARE NOT HARD TO FIND
If you know what to look for.

Lessons For Life Books
PUBLISHERS

L E S S O N S F O R L I F E B O O K S . C O M